Property Investment For Beginners

The Exclusive Real Estate Investment
Guide - How to benefit from the crisis,
leverage your capital and generate
long-term passive income incl.
Property Checklist

William K. Bradford

ISBN – 9798677555473

Table of Contents

Valavia
Romano.

About the Author

William K. Bradford has been working in property investment for nearly ten years and is highly experienced when it comes to maintaining properties, maximizing profits, and generating income in the long term. He have also guided a number of beginner property investors through their first investments, and has helped even more experienced investors plan their expansion and achieve greater success.

This is part of what prompted William K. Bradford to write this book - to give valuable help to a greater audience that he knows is guaranteed to educate and motivate investors of any caliber, whether beginner or professional. William K. Bradford learned much of what he knows from working in several investment firms, providing a variety of funds and investment services to prospective investors, including legal, portfolio management, and tax management services.

Property Investment for Beginners contains the bulk of this knowledge, and each method, plan, and strategy within has been proven over and over again to help achieve success in the property investment industry. William K. Bradford is certain that there is no better place to learn how to start investing in property than in the pages that follow.

He has curated each strategy to be as effective as possible, maximizing profits and minimizing vacancies, so that you get the most out of your properties. Of course, one can't expect to become an overnight millionaire, which is something that William K. Bradford has had to teach his apprentices countless times. Property investment takes a lot of work and determination, and this book will guide and motivate you to work as effectively as you can.

Chapter One:

Why Invest in Property?

There are far more reasons to invest in property than merely to generate income. While it is a lucrative market, the money is very rarely the be-all-end-all of real estate investment. Cash flow is important that much is certain, but there are so many other benefits that are often overlooked, which can have a significant impact on the investment experience.

When you choose your assets and priorities carefully, you can enjoy a cash flow that is predictable, tax advantages, excellent returns, and will be able to diversify your portfolio, while also being able to leverage your real estate to accumulate wealth. In this chapter, we are going to discuss a number of the many benefits to property investment, and how they can give you an advantage in the long run.

Cash flow

It goes without saying that the goal of every real estate investor that owns a rental property is to attain a positive cash flow on their investment property. Understanding the importance of cash flow and how it is calculated is vital, and finding solutions to cutting down the time it takes to calculate your cash flow can be even more important.

Calculating your properties' cash flow is perhaps the best way to determine its quality and estimating how profitable it can be. Most investment properties can have either a positive or negative cash flow, particularly with rental properties. If your goal is to make money by investing in real estate, you'll know that you have succeeded once you have one or more investment properties with a positive cash flow.

With a positive cash flow, your property makes money for you, regardless of how little the profit is. As long as you are achieving a positive cash flow with your property, you are safe. But, if your goal is to maximize your profits (which it probably is), you will need to understand what exactly cash flow is, and the ways that it influences your investment property.

What is Cash Flow, and how important is it for your Investment Property?

To put it simply, cash flow is the amount of profit that your investment property is making after you have calculated every expense that is related to your investment. Thus, a property with a positive cash flow is one that is producing more money than the sum of its expenses in one cycle.

Cycles are generally annually or monthly, but you'll find that the majority of property investors prefer the annual measurement for different reasons. The ability to calculate your investment property's cash flow is essential for successful real estate planning. This calculation helps estimate the possible expenses you may face and how they will affect you, as well as the influence they will have on the profitability of your real estate.

You'll be able to use these estimates to plan ahead and avoid situations in which your property will cause you to lose money suddenly. This is only possible because cash flow considers all of the expenses that can and will arise, even if you are unsure whether they will arise at all. This is where the difficulty occurs, as even though calculating cash flow may seem like a simple task, determining all of the possible expenses for your properties can be a hassle.

Later in this book, we are going to discuss how to calculate cash flow and cover a few of the possible expenses you may face when investing in property, especially as a novice.

Appreciation

Unfortunately, too many property investors do not know what to do with the potential price appreciation of their properties, so they simply do not take it into consideration. All too often, we tend only to focus on the cash flow from rental income, since it is arguably the easiest aspect to monitor. This makes it the only criterion that investors use to make decisions, and while it is the simpler method, it can also cost you hundreds of thousands of dollars.

Your rental property goal should not only be to achieve the highest cash flow. Instead, your goal should be the best risk-adjusted total return on your investment, assuming that the rental income covers your expenses. Merely assessing your cash flow to determine success and failure can be deceiving. You're able to more accurately determine what you need to do to achieve your financial goals when you analyze all of your profit centers, including cash flow, price appreciation, and tax savings.

Investment professionals have determined that real estate cycles will often repeat themselves every 10-20 years within a particular area or city. If you plan to maintain your properties for at least ten years and are familiar with the long-term historical appreciation rates, then you can expect a similar appreciation in the price of your property.

Diversifying your portfolio

Diversifying investment assets is vital to minimizing risk for every investor. By diversifying your property investment portfolio, you are essentially distributing your assets to reduce your overall risk of profit loss. To put it simply, if one property performs poorly during a cycle, but another performs better, your overall losses will be reduced.

How can you diversify your portfolio?

There are two main ways in which investors are able to diversify their property portfolio: by investing in different geographical locations, or by acquiring different property types. The latter is far more popular, as investing in another geographic location can be costly, and can make it challenging to prioritize.

Many amateur investors only consider apartments and houses when thinking about different types of properties. While building a diverse portfolio consisting of these assets can be effective, it is important to consider some of your other options as well. These options can include investing in townhouses and villas, in commercial property (directly or through a managed fund), or in residential development syndicates.

As with most things in the property investment industry, each of these properties come with their own pros and cons, so it's important to grasp each benefit and drawback, and how they work with your overall investment strategy. To put it into perspective, if you manage three homes in your portfolio, and they have high holding costs, it may be wise to buy an apartment or villa, since they generate higher cash flows thanks to their high rental incomes.

You could also diversify your portfolio by purchasing properties in different markets. You can do this by building a mixed portfolio consisting of properties in different capital city markets, whether in your home territory or not.

Most novice property investors will purchase their first few properties in their own capital city or region, generally in their own suburb, since they are familiar with the location. However, it is wise to begin looking at other markets after you have bought 3 - 4 properties in the same market, so that you may continue diversifying your portfolio.

This is extremely important because capital city property markets usually don't have aligned cycles. It means that property values in one market may be flourishing, while values in another market may plummet. This lets you distribute your risk by exposing yourself to several markets, offsetting any downfalls with increases.

Tax breaks and deductions

Property investment offers some excellent tax advantages that renting does not, but you'll need to understand how you can capitalize on these benefits. One of the greatest tax benefits for investors comes in the form of deductions, which are write-offs that include the costs associated with property tax, mortgage interest, operating expenses, and more.

What deductions can you make?

You are at liberty to deduct the necessary and regular expenses for managing and maintaining your property, as the property owner. These are considered *business finances* that will generally include property taxes, mortgage interest, maintenance, etc. As an investor, you're able to write off repairs, since they do not add value to a property, and serve only to keep them in good condition.

You can also deduct mortgage interest on your primary residences, and sometimes your secondary residence as well. Ensure that you carefully itemize your deductions. If you are thinking of starting a business, you should know that deductions can also come in the form of non-real estate activities, like using a home office. In most cases, you'll be able to deduct a portion of your home working expenses, like your phone bill and internet.

Investing in property can be beneficial in both the short and long term but determining what a meaningful goal is to you is what's most important. You also need to continually remind yourself that hardly anyone becomes an overnight millionaire through property investment. Doing so will help keep you motivated and inspired and will propel you towards reaching your goals.

Chapter Two:

A Diverse Market

As we've mentioned before, there is a lot more to property investment than simply owning a house or apartment and leasing it out. There are many other kinds of properties available to prospective investors, and there are several different ways in which one can invest in a property and generate income from it. Since this is a complete beginner's guide, we're going to cover the simpler investments you can make when entering the real estate field.

The different real estate investments

Residential

Residential properties are structures such as apartment buildings, houses, vacation houses, and townhouses, where an individual or group pays you to live in. The length of the stay, as well as the rent amount due each month, is determined by the rental or lease agreement. Most residential leases in the United States work off of a twelve-month basis.

Residential properties are perhaps the safest investments that new investors can make, which also makes them the most popular. They are generally less expensive to acquire than most of the other property types that we will discuss, depending on the area they are located in and the condition that they are in when you purchase them.

Residential properties usually also require less hands-on maintenance, since the tenants that stay there will generally keep it in good condition. However, you cannot rely on tenants to do this all the time, and some tenants may even let the property deteriorate over the course of their stay. It will then be up to you to restore the property once their lease has ended, which can cost you precious time and money.

However, you'll find that most tenants avoid letting this happen, so it's quite a rare scenario.

Commercial

Commercial properties are also fairly popular real estate investment options and consist mainly of skyscrapers and office buildings. If you were to acquire or construct a small building with individual offices within, you could lease each individual office to small business owners and companies who would pay rent to use the property. It is quite common for commercial properties to use multi-year leases since they can provide a stable cash flow, and sometimes even protect the owner from the decline of rental rates.

However, prospective investors should always keep in mind that markets will fluctuate, and rental rates may significantly increase over a short period. But you might be unable to raise your rental rates if your commercial property is bound by older agreements. Commercial buildings generally require a greater level of involved maintenance, as they are quite a bit larger than residential properties.

Retail

Retail properties include things like strip malls, shopping malls, and other smaller retail storefronts. Similarly to residential properties, retail locations do not require much hands-on maintenance from the owner, as tenants generally like to keep their stores as clean and orderly as possible.

In some cases, you, as the owner will receive a percentage of the income generated by the tenant store's sales, in addition to the base rent, which will provide an incentive for the tenant to keep the property as pristine as possible. Retail property investment, especially in smaller storefronts, can be unpredictable, as the tenant relies solely on the sales they make to pay their rent to you. If a store runs out of stock or loses customers, they will not be able to pay their rent, and they will have to move out.

This is why it's recommended that beginner investors avoid jumping into a retail investment, and instead opt for residential or commercial investments, where a stable income is almost guaranteed.

Industrial

Perhaps the most lucrative property investment, industrial real estate, includes storage units, warehouses, car washes, and any other special-purpose property that generates sales from customers that make use of the facility. For example, if you were to acquire a car wash, you could install some coin-operated vacuum cleaners, which would increase the return on your investment.

Mixed-Use

As the name suggests, mixed-use properties are lots that combine any of the categories mentioned above into one project. These types of properties are popular amongst investors that have access to significant access and cash, as they have a level of diversification that is built-in, which, as we have mentioned in the previous chapter, is important to control risk.

The different ways to invest in property

There are a couple of other ways to successfully invest in property other than becoming a landlord, like house flipping or real estate investment groups. Let's discuss some of them:

[handwritten note: Start with 1/2 flats as a base, rather houses rather than flats]

Becoming a Landlord

By far the most popular way to invest in real estate, becoming a landlord ensures that you have total control over your property, and how it generates income for you. However, you will need a substantial sum of capital to be able to finance some of the initial costs for maintenance, and also to cover any vacant months (or months where your property is not generating income). Rental properties can provide a regular income to landlords, while also using leverage to maximize their available capital.

What's more, many of the expenses that are associated with rental properties are tax-deductible, and most gains can be offset with losses with other investments. In the ideal situation, rental properties can appreciate in value over the duration of their mortgages, which leave landlords with an asset more valuable than when they started.

The drawback comes in when we consider maintenance. Unless you employ a company to manage your properties for you, rentals will often cause headache after headache. In the worst scenarios, unruly tenants could cause damage to your property. Additionally, in certain rental market environments, you as a landlord will need to charge less rent or bear vacancies so that you can cover expenses until the situation improves.

On a more positive note, as soon as the mortgage is paid off in full, most of the rent becomes profit entirely.

House Flipping

House flipping is more for folks who have significant experience in real estate marketing and evaluation, as well as expertise in renovation. To flip houses, you will need some capital, and will also need to be able to oversee or perform repairs as they are needed.

There is a shorter period during which effort and capital are tied up in a property when flipping houses, though, depending on the conditions of the market, you can receive significant returns, even in shorter time frames. However, trading real estate requires a more in-depth knowledge of the market, and there is a certain degree of pure luck involved, making it a field better-suited to more experienced property investors.

Real Estate Investment Groups

REIGs are perfect for those that wish to own rental properties without needing to deal with running them. They require a 'capital cushion' and sufficient funding and are a far less involved approach to property investment that can still provide appreciation and income.

There is, unfortunately, a risk of vacancy when working with real estate investment groups, whether it is specific to the owner or distributed throughout the group. In theory, such groups are a safe way to invest in property, but in practice, they are susceptible to similar fees that the mutual fund industry faces.

Furthermore, REIGs are occasionally private investments that dishonest management teams use to swindle money from their investors. Therefore, you will need to be meticulous when choosing a real estate investment group to avoid the risk of being scammed as much as possible.

REIGs are similar to mutual funds that invest in rental real estate. Standard real estate investment groups lease a property in the name of the investor, and each unit pools a part of the rent as a kind of safeguard against any occasional vacancies that may occur. This allows you to receive a bit of income, even if your property is vacant. There should be enough to cover costs, provided that the vacancy rates for the pooled units do not get too high.

It's clear to see that the property investment industry is exceptionally diverse, and there are plenty of options available out there to prospective investors. The different investment and property types that we have mentioned above one just a few of many, and could write a separate book on each of them. Choosing the right one to start with can make or break your property investment career, so it's recommended that you consider one that we mentioned above.

Chapter Three:

Creating a Business Plan

All successful businesses start with a plan, and pretty much anyone who achieves great success started out with one that is solid and comprehensive. Even if you plan something simple, it is still a statement of what you intend to do with your business, and how you plan on making it profitable. The vast majority of novice property investors looking to enter the industry, start without even a basic plan, which ultimately leads to failure.

It often feels as though we're sitting around and wasting our time creating a plan when we could be out there looking at properties and start making money. But it's important to realize that almost everyone who does not begin with a plan ends up disappointed and dissatisfied, regardless of the amount of time and effort they put in.

What is a property investment business plan, and what does it look like?

There's no need to create hundreds of pages of fancy charts and projections when developing your property investment business plan. On the contrary, the best business plan would be one so simple that it could fit on a single page so that you're able to memorize it and use it to motivate each decision you make.

In order to achieve such simplicity, you will have to think long and hard about your priorities. Below is an example of what your business plan could look like:

Current Budget	$100 000
Goal Profits	$50 000
Current Debt	$75 000
Current properties owned	1
Current Property Types	Residential, Commercial
Goal Properties	3

Of course, your plan does not have to be identical to this, and you should take the time to personalize it to your goals, making it as brief or extensive as you'd like. The key is creating a plan that is easy for you to understand, interpret, and follow. Your goals should also be realistic, as setting unattainable goals will inevitably leave you feeling dejected and without motivation.

Where are you currently?

It's impossible to plan ahead if you don't know where you're starting from. Determining your point of origin is the easiest part of creating a business plan because it consists of information that you either already know, or that is easy for you to learn. You need to consider things like the amount of money that you have available to invest, how much of your savings can be put towards property investment in the future, and the time you're able to invest each week or month.

The thing that makes this part of your business plan difficult is the fact that you need to be honest to yourself about what you can commit, and knowing yourself well enough to see what your strengths are. Knowing how

24

much money you have to invest should not be a problem, but you may want to consult with a mortgage broker to see your borrowing options.

This will help you figure out your total investment figure. Brokers are also able to inform you about the options that are available to you regarding releasing equity from your own home if that is something you wish to do. You should also consider keeping an emergency fund in cash and deduct that amount from your total investment budget.

Having around half a year's expenses in the bank at all times will act as a safeguard if your plan ever fails. Pouring every cent to your name into your investments very rarely ends well - you still want to be able to pay your bills.

Where do you want to go?

Now that you have an idea of your starting point, it's time to look at where you want to be in the future, or what are your **goals?** Of course, you want to be secure or rich, or you want to build a future. Who doesn't? But you'll need to know what that means and what it looks like to you in terms of cash. You also need to figure out when you want to achieve these goals.

There is a lot of thought involved in figuring these things out the proper way. Being general is not useful - you need to take an honest look at your ideal lifestyle and come up with a figure that is truly meaningful to you, regardless of how big or small it is. The same also goes for the time you want to take to reach your goals, as it can drastically influence even your most basic investment decisions.

Here's an example to help put things into perspective:

Property A provides a return of 12% on your investment, but it is highly unlikely that it will ever increase in value.

On the other hand, *Property B* provides an 8% return on your investment, but could possibly double in value during the next decade.

If your goal is to generate a specific income each month within four years, then *Property A* will probably be your best choice. It is unlikely for any major growth to occur during that time, so you will need to prioritize money in your bank now.

what is our goal timeline

Otherwise, if your goal spans more than a decade, you would likely find *Property B* to be more beneficial. Investing in this property is a small risk in terms of growth on capital, but there is a lot of time for it to happen, and when it eventually does happen, your returns will make the higher rental income from *Property A* look like pocket change.

By this point in the planning process, you may realize that the gap between where you are and where you want to be, seems almost too vast. It probably seems impossible to reach your goals with the resources you currently have at your disposal. This is why it is now time to start thinking of a strategy you will use to pursue and achieve your goal.

Investment strategies and how you can use them

When you are creating a property investment business plan, you have to take into consideration which kind of investment strategy will suit your goals the best. We are going to take a look at a few strategies that are **proven** to be effective, as well as some of their pros and cons.

Professional Single Lets

This is by far the most commonly used investment strategy and succeeds the most often as well. Buying a property and renting it out to a tenant can generate income in one of two ways - the growth in the property's capital value over time, and the monthly rental income after the deduction of expenses.

Professional single lets are the 'traditional' buy-to-let method, which involves renting out a property to a working family or individual as a single unit. It has been around for ages and is the simplest form of property investment there is. You just need to get your calculations correct the first time, buy in a good area or region, rent the property to a tenant, and ensure that they are gladly paying their rent on time.

This is a gross simplification, but this is all that is at the core of professional single let renting. While we are going to cover a few more advanced property investment strategies, this is the one that most property investors use and is one of the most effective as well, which lends to its popularity.

Pros:

- Simplest investment strategy

- Very little management time required   *Not neccessarily!*

- Easy to acquire mortgages for

- Predictable returns

Cons:

- Lower returns than other strategies

Holiday Lets

As you may have guessed, holiday lets are properties that are rented out over short periods to holidaymakers. They are also sometimes called 'serviced accommodations,' which are essentially the same things, but with a target demographic of business travelers in urban areas. There is quite a bit of intersection between these terms, and their basic structures are the same - the difference lies in the type of customer that is targeted.

If you're able to achieve a high occupancy level with this strategy, the profits can be incredible. A cottage near the sea, for example, can be quite easy to fill up during the warmer months of the year, but you can make even more money if you're able to keep it occupied throughout the rest of the year, even if you have to lower your rates somewhat.

The only real downside to this strategy is that it requires pretty much round-the-clock work, with frequent occupancy changes and marketing to consider. It can also be quite challenging to find a mortgage that will permit lets for such short terms, so the return on your investment might be even lower with a high rental income due to reduced leverage.

Pros:

- No secure tenure = no need for evictions

- High occupancy yields high returns

- Better tax deductions

Cons:

- Requires year-round work

HMOs

In essence, HMOs are shared homes that are rented per room to unrelated tenants. There are a number of separate definitions for what exactly constitutes an HMO, but we'll stick with the basic definition for the purpose of this guide.

On average, renting out a property by the room can generate more revenue than if you were to rent it out as a whole. However, they also come with higher costs, since HMOs are usually furnished, and include bills - and there is often more wear and tear to these properties.

Managing an HMO can definitely be more time consuming, meaning your letting agent fees could be higher, or you as a landlord may need to be more involved.

Even after you have taken these extra costs into consideration, HMOs can offer a higher yield, which has caused them to surge in popularity over the last few years. However, this means that councils have also taken more action to regulate them by increasing the types of HMOs that need to be licensed, making existing regulations more thorough, and denying access to the development of new HMOs in certain areas.

Pros:

- Diverse stream of income

- Greater yield than single lets

Cons:

- More regulations

- Requires more thorough management

There are many more property investment strategies out there that come with their own benefits and drawbacks - those mentioned above are merely the most popular and have the highest rates of success, especially for investors just entering the market. While you are under no obligation to make use of one of these strategies are highly recommend that you do, as they are guaranteed to be profitable.

We should go to auctions …? Just to observe

Chapter Four:

Investing in Your First Property

Now that you are familiar with the very basics of property investment, it's time to learn how to invest in your first property. Making your first real estate investment is both an exciting and stressful time. It can be incredibly taxing to move from one house show to the next in between your daily tasks, but signing your name on the sales contract is one of the most satisfying feelings ever, and makes it all worth it.

In this chapter, we're going to look at how you can achieve your investment dreams through careful planning and consideration. The process is fairly simple, but it requires plenty of effort and critical thinking.

Get out of debt

Easier said than done, right? This first step is the most important in this process since your credit score is the first thing that is evaluated when applying for a home loan. If you are still deep in debt, it might be quite challenging for you to receive approval for your bond.

If you still find yourself struggling to repay your credit card accounts, student loans, or medical bills, then investing in real estate might not be the wise thing to do at this stage in your life. Consider getting advice from a debt counselor on how you can pay off your debt in the shortest amount of time, then consider property investment.

If you currently earn enough money to pay off all of your outstanding debts, and the monthly mortgage costs and those related as well, then you are free to start considering acquiring your first investment property.

Understand the difference between your first home and an investment property

This may be obvious to some, but it's worth mentioning anyway. After all, this is a guide for total beginners. There is a very clear difference between making your first property investment and buying your primary residence. The former will, hopefully, provide you with a constant flow of income through rental payment and a profit once you sell it, while the latter is the place in which you'll live permanently.

Understanding this difference *before* you begin searching for a property is vital because there are several various factors that you'll have to take into consideration before you make your purchase. These factors will include things like proximity to general services, work, and family, or the number of rooms you need in a property.

All of these things will have some impact on your decision-making process when buying your primary residence but will probably not influence your decision when acquiring an investment property. Investment properties will often be the cheaper of these two options since they won't have to meet all the requirements for an ideal home.

You will also need to pay the Capital Gains Tax when selling an investment property, which you will not have to pay if and when you decide to sell your primary residence. You can also make the distinction based on your emotions - buying your primary residence is more of an emotional decision than buying an investment property, as you'll be considering the space that your loved ones will be living in.

Realize that managing a property requires a lot of effort

As we have discussed a few times before, being a landlord can and will be a very time-consuming task, especially if you work a full-time job as well. If you thought that finding a property was difficult, wait until you have to start managing one.

Tenants can be quite demanding sometimes, especially if your property has a faulty feature or fixture - they'll probably want it fixed immediately. This is fair since you would probably want your landlord to fix any problems your rented property might have as well. You will encounter at least one tenant during your property investment career that will be late on their rent payments, and sometimes not pay rent at all.

This can be incredibly frustrating, especially if you only own one investment property that is the sole source of your cash flow. But it's important to be patient, and hiring a rental agent that acts as the middleman between you and your tenant/s can help ease some of the stress. Living on-site can be beneficial as well, as you'll be more inclined to keep your property pristine, and it could help reduce travel costs as well.

Pay attention to location

You've probably heard the phrase 'location, location, location' at least once in your life, but do you know what it actually means? Most people don't, because there are several factors that determine whether or not a location can be considered 'good', most of which are very subjective.

The safest bet is to choose a location that is close to amenities like stores and public transports. Places near universities are ideal as well, because most students will rent your property for the duration of their time studying at the university, and their parents will generally provide some personal guarantees on the rent.

Finding a good location will ensure that you receive some good returns on your investment, and can improve the resale value of your property as well. Gentrified areas, or areas that have been developed to be comfortable to the middle class are also becoming popular amongst property investors since properties within them cost less to acquire and appreciate in value faster. Remember to only explore options in locations that you can comfortably afford, or you risk putting yourself in a dangerous situation, however tempting it may be.

Examine the economic cycle at present

The economic cycle can be thought of in three stages, and first-time property investors should pay careful attention to these stages, and the cycle as a whole. The first stage in the economic cycle is the **Recession Stage,** which is the best and scariest time to acquire property. Unemployment and inflation are high in this stage, and the demand for rental properties tends to decline.

The next stage is the **Recovery Stage,** in which rental rates begin to increase once more, and the number of vacancies starts to decrease. Finally, we reach the third and final stage, called the **Peak Stage.** In this stage, you'll notice an increase in interest rates, an increase in the number of new projects, and a rise in inflation. Some markets can experience a leveling of prices and increased rates of vacancy.

Source service providers that are trustworthy and professional

As a property investor, one of your responsibilities will be to accumulate a list of professional service providers that you can trust. These should include accountants, lawyers, and tradesmen like plumbers and electricians. The easiest way to do this is to talk to your friends.

They are likely to know at least one person who can help you and will be able to provide you with their contact details if you just ask. You could also turn to the internet, which has a wealth of property professionals looking for clients. Just make sure that you read any business reviews they may have, and see what other people are saying and if they can be trusted.

Or, if this all sounds a little too challenging or time-consuming, you could hire a property manager, though they might be quite costly for a prospective property investor just entering the field.

Acquire financing for your property

If you are going to pay for your investment property in cash, then you don't need to follow this step. Otherwise, you will need to find a way to get money for your purchase. Financing a primary residence and financing an investment property are two very different processes. You will need excellent qualifications since lenders generally consider mortgages for investment properties riskier than loans on properties occupied by the owner.

You have a few options for financing your investment property, and you should consider having a preapproval for a loan regardless of which you choose. Otherwise, you should have financing secured *before* you begin browsing properties.

broker advice

Conventional financing - this blanket term refers to a mortgage that is obtained from a bank and is backed up by your personal qualifications. There are a number of factors that determine the requirements for conventional financing, like your credit score, the property type, and your employment status. Conventional loans are generally the most effective way to go if you are able to qualify for one.

[handwritten margin note: Is our current situ likely to adversely effect?]

Asset-based loans - this is the main alternative to conventional loans, and, as the name suggests, the qualifications for this loan depend on the asset in question (the investment property in this case) rather than the qualifications of the borrower. In other words, asset-based lenders will check your credit score to see if you are eligible, but they will not look at your income, debts, or employment status.

The main condition is that your property will need to generate enough cash flow to cover the payments for the mortgage, with a realistic cushion as well. The lender will make use of what is known as the DSCR, or the Debt Service Coverage Ratio.

Choose a mortgage type and develop a comprehensive lease

There are several options available to you when deciding on a type of mortgage, like paying the loan back over either 15 or 30 years or having a fixed or adjustable rate. In the case of most mortgages, you will be required to provide a deposit of at least 5% towards the property.

The goal is to pay the least amount possible upfront since your payments will be lower if your deposit is a large sum. You should also keep in mind that your mortgage costs might not fully be covered by your rental price.

After you have acquired your first investment property, you will begin the next cycle of property investment, which mostly consists of finding a tenant that is suitable for your property. Be sure to draft a legal lease agreement with your lawyer when doing so. *Is this tax deductable?*

This lease should include things like a summary of the fees such as water and electricity, policies regarding pets, subletting, and misconduct, etc., penalties for breaching the lease, as well as methods and due dates for payments.

Below is a checklist that you can use to determine whether or not you meet the requirement that you'll need to invest in your first property.

Property Checklist

- ❑ Debt-free

- ❑ Know the difference between a primary residence and an investment property

- ❑ Prepared for the effort required of a landlord

- ❑ Found an ideal location

- ❑ Considered and understand the current economic cycle

- ❑ Sourced professional, trustworthy service providers (lawyers, accountants, electricians, etc.)

- ❑ Sourced secure financing OR have sufficient finances already

- ❑ Settled on a mortgage type

- ❑ Developed a comprehensive lease

- ❑ Acquired my first investment property!

Once you've checked every box on this list, you'll be ready to acquire your first property and then move onto the next chapter, in which we'll discuss how you can generate as much profit as possible.

Chapter Five:

Maximizing Your Profits

If there's one thing that we know for certain, it's that you are interested in the property investment industry for one thing: PROFIT. We all want to be rich, and while real estate won't make us millionaires overnight, it can get us a lot of money in a relatively short amount of time. Your investment should be generating at least a 6%-8% return. *regular return*

The three main factors that will have a positive impact on the profits that you earn are **occupancy, maintenance,** and **on-time payments.** This includes every rental property you have in your portfolio, regardless of whether you manage them yourself, or via a management company. If you are using a managing company, and they aren't helping you make *% returns, then you need to review the way they are managing your properties.

Key Question: Why aren't you achieving maximum profits?

There are a few things that are likely preventing you from achieving that 6-8% return margin. We are going to discuss them below, and how you can remedy them and maximize your profits.

Inadequate tenant screening, or none at all

Tenant screening should be at the top of your list of priorities as a rental property owner. Your investment can only ever be profitable if you are leasing your properties to tenants that pay their rent on time and do not cause damage to your real estate. You could even consider collecting a security deposit to cover the property damage costs, but the overhead and time required to perform property repairs will chew through your income.

There are a couple of options available to monitor the bill-paying habits of your future tenants. You can view their credit reports, assess their tendency to follow the rules by browsing their criminal background and contacting previous landlords, and review their bank statements to see how much money they earn.

You would be shocked at just how many landlords don't take advantage of these basic practices for screening tenants. There are quality background checks and tenant credit checks for as little as $15, and this small investment is well worth it to prevent any potential loss of rent from a tenant who does not may and any dangerous activity that you may have to deal with.

Tenants that are responsible, and that have a verifiable bill-paying and rule-complying history will ensure that you have a positive tenant-landlord relationship, which subsequently maximizes the amount of cash you receive.

Online rent payments mean fewer late payments

Stop wasting time with those pesky deposit checks and have your tenants pay online, which will also avoid sitting through excuses like 'it was lost in the mail'. Smart investors value their time just as much as they do their other assets. There exist various software solutions that are designed to enable renters to streamline their rental management. One of the best and newest of these technologies is the ability to make rental payments online.

Not only do online rent payments make the rent collection process exquisitely simple, but they also make life easier for your tenants as well. It may sound silly, but the rent check that your tenants pay is normally the largest bill they pay each month, and writing that check out can be stressful, even emotional sometimes. Online payments can lower this stress significantly, especially when using automatic payment systems.

You should also ensure that your automatic bill payments are set up as well, so you don't miss any bills that you might have otherwise. You can also sometimes negotiate a discount with online services for paying your bills, which will reduce your overall operating costs and increase your profits even more.

Relying on tenants to maintain your properties

This problem is no more your fault than it is your tenants. People are forgetful, particularly in the rushed working world of today. Your tenants might not be familiar with what they need to do to keep a home free of damage via routine maintenance, especially if they are young adults.

You have no control over how your tenants will use features or fixtures in your property, especially regarding appliances like refrigerators and thermostats. Even if you are totally confident that all your bases are covered by requiring tenants to perform basic maintenance, they will probably still forget.

That's why it is up to you to invest some money and time into routine service and maintenance checkups on the main appliances in your properties. This will extend the life of such appliances, like ovens, air conditioning, washers, dryers, and so on. The same can be said for seasonal maintenance.

It's one thing to state in your lease that tenants should trim the trees and clean the driveway, but you will face a much more costly bill if they fail to do so than if you were to send over a seasonal landscaper annually, who would be able to perform these maintenance tasks. You need to make your maintenance expectations crystal-clear to your tenants, and they need to know exactly what they are expected to take care of.

You should also remind them every now and then about when and how they need to do these tasks. Set reminders on your phone's calendar for every season to do things like change an air filter or clean the gutters. Allow your tenants to easily and conveniently submit requests for maintenance if you're looking to keep damage to your property at a minimum. Software that offers a tenant portal online is one easy solution, as it will let your renters submit maintenance requests straight from their smartphones. The easier it is for tenants to report maintenance issues, the more likely they are to take the time to report them.

Increase the rent

This may seem obvious but increasing the rent that tenants will pay to stay on your investment properties will increase the profits that you make. Increases in rent keep your property within the market value price, allow you to reach rates that are profitable, and help you stay on top of your expenses.

The key to increasing your rent successfully is by getting as little backlash from your tenants as you can. The increase should meet the demands of the market, but it should not be so extreme that your tenants are not able to afford it and move out, which would result in a vacancy and a decrease in profits. Building regular increases in rent into your lease agreement is the easiest way to present approachable increases.

Legal doc (handwritten annotation)

By doing this, you are allowing your tenants to prepare for these living expenses raises so that they can budget accordingly.

Permit pets

The vast majority of us have pets, and we all know how difficult it is to find housing that is pet-friendly. As an investor, you are given the opportunity to capitalize on this demand for housing that accommodates pets, by allowing tenants to have pets on your property, with rules that are clearly outlined, and a higher rent amount.

You could possibly charge a monthly rent for pets on the property if your tenant owns any, which is an easy way to get additional income from that property. If the pet ever causes damage to your property, which is very unlikely, then you will still be able to deduct the necessary amount from the tenant's security deposit.

However, you should know that **emotional support animals and service animals are not considered pets, and you are not allowed to charge additional fees for these types of animals.**

Offer more services

If you own a triplex, fourplex, or multi-family property, you might be able to increase your profits via coin-operated laundry machines. Providing an on-site laundry facility can make your property more appealing, especially if the property does not provide an in-unit washer or dryer.

You can lease these machines from major appliance companies, or you could buy the machines yourself and keep all of the profits, but you'd need to maintain them yourself as well. Also, keep in mind any other laundry facilities in the neighborhood, as well as water costs, to ensure that having an on-site laundry facility will benefit both you and your tenants.

Keep up-to-date with maintenance

One of the best and most effective ways to increase the lifespan and profitability of your properties is to keep them routinely maintained. As an investor, it is your responsibility to be very diligent when it comes to maintenance since you are not always going to be on your property, ensuring that routine tasks are being done.

Landlords also need to inform their tenants about how important it is that they maintain the property to some extent. This should all be outlined in your lease agreement, even if doing so may seem obvious. Being diligent with routine seasonal maintenance will save you a lot of money, and will help you avoid the cost of contractors who will need to fix a feature or appliance that would have lasted longer had you otherwise maintained them properly.

Work with a team that you trust

There will be times when you have to hire a professional to fix something, regardless of how well you and your tenants worked to maintain your property.

Knowing the right vendors and contractors and being able to get a hold of them quickly, will help keep your costs as low as possible when an issue with maintenance arises.

Having good relationships with electricians, plumbers, painters, and various other home maintenance professionals and vendors will give you quick and easy access to the right services when they are needed. If your tenant contacts you with an emergency regarding maintenance, you will be able to call the appropriate maintenance professional and can pay them a favorable price.

The last thing you want to do is call around in an effort to find someone who is available when you need them to handle your emergency. It is at this point that maintenance can become incredibly expensive.

By now, you may have noticed that the best way to maximize your profits is not to increase the amount of money you are receiving each month, but rather to decrease your costs for the upkeep of your properties. Keep your expenses low and reserve fund topped-up by taking the time to screen tenants and eliminating potential damage to your property.

Chapter Six:

Maintaining Your Property

Taking care of your investment properties is just as important as acquiring them, if not more. Your real estate needs meticulous care and special attention to become successful and stay that way, as with most things in life. We're going to take a look at some of the things you can do to ensure that your properties are always in the best condition they can be, and how you can maintain a consistent occupancy.

Inspecting the interior and exterior of your properties

A well-kept property that is free of any kind of damage will help raise your profits and keep good tenants. As we discussed in the previous chapter, some maintenance tasks are inevitable, and your properties will become damaged in some way throughout the course of your investment career. Being able to closely inspect your properties for any damages, no matter how minor they may be, is a vital skill that can spell the difference between a good landlord, and an excellent one.

Be sure to **check all of the windows** and see if they are sealed correctly, with no gaps in any of the panes or fillings. If there are gaps, fill them. Doing so will save you plenty of money in the future that would otherwise have to be spent on heat loss and damage caused by moisture.

Check the roof for any tiles or shingles that may be missing, and mold or moss, and for any flashing that has been damaged. While these may seem like minor things that don't require immediate attention, they can cause some serious damage that will cost you a small fortune to repair. You should also check if there are any tree limbs that have grown onto your roof. If there are, cut them off, so that they don't scratch the roof, or fall off. They are also quite unattractive and can be a deterrent for tenants.

Look for any **broken tree limbs** or **trees with fungal growths.** These things can be dangerous to the tenant living on the property, so you'll want to deal with them immediately. Also, make sure that the lawn is healthy and that the grass is mowed regularly - this will let any potential tenants know that you are dedicated to keeping your property maintained.

Ensure that **the exterior walls are always painted** to prevent any sun or moisture damage to the property. If your house doesn't look good, nobody will want to live in it.

Regarding the interior of the property, you will want to ensure that there are **smoke detectors** in the kitchen and that they always have new, working batteries. Non-functional smoke detectors pose a serious threat to tenants, so keeping them up and running is essential.

The **water heater should be kept clean** at all times. Drain it and remove any dirt on a regular basis, especially if your property is located in an area with a lot of sediment in the water.

Inspect the heating and cooling system regularly, and make sure that there are no plants or fungi growing around its filters. They can restrict the flow of air and can damage the system beyond repair, which will cost you a lot of money to replace.

Keeping your tenants happy and satisfied

Keeping your tenants happy is just as important as keeping your property in pristine condition, with the latter having a major impact on the former. If your tenants are satisfied, they will be more inclined to keep your property maintained, which saves you the hassle and cost of having to repair damages yourself.

A simple checkup every once in a while to see how things are going, or asking if there's anything that they need will be more than enough. Showing your tenants that you care about their comfort and that you are willing to help them through any property-related stresses that their satisfaction is your priority will make all the difference in the world.

This also boosts your reputation with future tenants and will make you a magnet for prospective renters. Make sure that you respond to their maintenance requests. One of the leading causes of tenants moving out is dissatisfaction, so keep them pleased as much as possible.

Follow the Landlord-Tenant law

The landlord-tenant law outlines the rights and obligations that each party has regarding a rental property. Both the tenant and the landlord will need to know the basics of renting a home, how to pay or collect security deposits, and much more.

Newer landlords will likely need help working out their tax deductions or figuring out how to go about evicting a tenant because of unpaid rent. On the other hand, tenants might need assistance with understanding their right to safety as a tenant, how their security deposits are returned, and whether they are able to sublet a property.

Following the landlord-tenant law will aid you in maintaining your investment property and correctly managing it. It provides a basic structure for both you and your tenant so that neither of you makes any mistakes, and you're able to keep your property in good condition. Under this law, the tenant is obligated to maintain the property that they are renting, which is a huge bonus for landlords, especially those who have a number of properties that require micromanaging.

Hire a property manager

This may be a bit of a costly task for beginner property investors, but if you are able to afford a property manager, you can gain access to a host of benefits. By now, you will have noticed that taking care of a property is a lot of work, and it can often feel overwhelming.

Property managers help relieve some of this stress by essentially maintaining your investment real estate for you. Hiring one is a big decision to make, as the services they provide come with a steep price tag attached, but you'll be saving yourself a lot of time if you do. Property managers can do everything from handling the rent to touching up the interior and exterior of your property.

Renovations and improvements

Prospective tenants are continually looking for new and developed properties available for rent. As a landlord, it is essential that you always consider ways that you can renovate and improve your investment properties. Doing so will increase their value and will attract tenants who may be interested in renting your property.

Some renovating ideas include fixing up the bathrooms by either replacing the old fixtures with new and improved versions or changing the appearance of the bathroom to something more modern. You could remove the carpeting in the house and switch it out for hardwood flooring, which is more attractive and hygienic since there will be no fibers for dirt to cling to.

You could also consider upgrading the kitchen with newer appliances, and add some more non-essential ones like a coffee machine. Kitchen and bathroom renovation can be either very cheap or extremely expensive, but both options will increase the value of your property.

Why is it important to maintain your investment property?

Keeping your property in top shape has a number of benefits. The first and most obvious is that it will help you avoid any additional costs. Ensuring that you fix a problem early will reduce the number of problems you'll have to deal with in the future significantly, which subsequently reduces the number of your expenses.

Keeping a strict maintenance routine will let both you and your tenant know that your real estate is always ready for service. Keeping your property maintained will also attract good tenants. If your property is poorly kept when you are trying to get a tenant to move in, you might start to attract unruly tenants who could damage your real estate. A good property can also yield more rental income as well.

Chapter Seven:

Managing Your Finances

We've discussed profits, expenses, and income in great detail so far, but now it's time to take things one step further and talk about how you should be managing your finances to become a successful property investor. Whether your investment goals are long-term or short-term, you should always look at your investment over the long term, using a ten-year view, especially if your strategy is to buy and maintain property.

Finance is just as important as choosing a property, as we've said time and time again, and it can often even be more important. The volume of property that you're able to acquire depends on how much financing you can borrow or generate - if you don't get your finances ordered, you may bottleneck your ability to expand and diversify your investment portfolio.

More often than not, you are going to need to borrow money from a bank in order to finance a property purchase. This amount of debt that you will require is also known as **the level of gearing.** The higher this level, the higher your risk of financial troubles, should you lose a tenant, or if interest rates were to increase. The main advantage that gearing provides is that the interest you pay is tax-deductible, making the investment more tax-efficient overall.

Some finance tips

The advice below can be applied anywhere in your property investment career, whether you are just starting out or whether you have been in the industry for a decade. Properly managing your finances will only ever be beneficial in both the short term and long term. Here are a few ways that you can manage your finances:

Consolidate your debts

We've already discussed this matter in *Chapter Four,* but ensuring that all of your debt is paid off before you invest in a property, whether it's your first or your tenth, will allow you to borrow more money from the bank. This subsequently lets you purchase more high-end properties, or put more cash towards renovating and improving your existing properties, which increases their value and causes them to appreciate quicker.

If you have multiple outstanding loans, make sure that you pay off the ones with the highest interest rates first, since they cost you the most in the long run. High-interest loans also impact your borrowing capacity the most, which is why getting them out of the way should be one of your priorities.

Cancel unused credit cards and reduce credit card limits

If truly honest, credit cards are poison. Yes, they're useful, and yes, they can get us out of a tight situation in a pinch, but they can also often lead to some crippling debt, especially if you get into the habit of overspending. Reducing the limit on your credit card or cards can make a massive difference to the amount of money you are able to borrow for your property. If you have some credit cards that you are not using, you should consider canceling them, since lenders will take your credit cards into account when calculating how much you are able to borrow, even if you aren't using them.

I recommend having a maximum of two credit cards. Try to have one for spending on improving your existing properties, while using the other to acquire more property. This will be a form of financial management without much planning.

Use different lenders

Convenience and loyalty are the main reasons that people tend to stick with the same lender each time they need to borrow money. However, this ultimately decreases the amount of money that you are allowed to borrow and increases your risks. When one lender funds your entire portfolio, they begin to assess your properties a whole instead of individually.

Using separate lenders lets you track down the best deal possible, keeping you in total control of your assets, and, most important, y increases your borrowing capabilities.

Plan!

There's a reason that I dedicated an entire chapter to creating a business plan (see: *Chapter Three).* As the old saying goes, 'fail to plan, and you plan to fail.' This is especially true in the property investment industry since you are often working with large sums of money that need to be carefully spent.

As with any other successful business, investors need to develop detailed and comprehensive plans that outline the strategies that will allow them to grow their property portfolio. Not only that, but it will help them plan and manage the finances that will be needed to achieve their goals, and should provide an analysis of cash flow and how costs like debt are going to be taken care of.

Avoid cross-collateralization

Cross-collateralization is the term that is used when the collateral for one loan becomes the collateral for another, separate loan. If you were to borrow a home loan and use your house as security, or borrow a car loan and use your car as security, from the same bank, those assets could be used as *cross-collaterals* for both loans, and so on.

This can cause some tremendous issues when your properties start to appreciate in value, and you want to release some of the equity that has been generated. The lender has your assets all tied up, meaning that if you wanted to consult another lender that offers a better deal, your current lender might not partly discharge their mortgage so that you could refinance the property.

Additionally, if you wish to sell a portion of your property portfolio to help consolidate any financial troubles you may be having, the lender might call in their loans. This would mean you would have to sell the properties in such a way that would leave you at a loss.

Have a redraw facility or a line of credit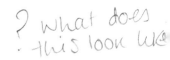

Focusing on the positives is important, but you need to make sure that you are fully prepared for the negatives. Time and time again I see far too few investors heed this advice, and issues end up catching them completely off guard. Many investors don't do enough to ensure that they are protecting their cash flow if times get tough.

By properly setting up a reserve of cash from the very beginning of your career through a line of credit or a redraw facility, you are creating a buffer or cushion for yourself that will give you peace of mind and help you through any financial troubles you may face.

Examine your security regularly

Providing your lenders with too much security is a surefire way to restrict your potential as an investor. Lenders will always tell you that there is no such thing as too much security, but you should review the values of your properties every year. Also, have them re-valued with a bank whenever you notice an increase of around 7%.

Over time, you will be able to remove the security from one of your investment properties, or from your home, granting you more independence and freedom of movement.

Financial considerations

When buying an investment property, there are a couple of things you need to ask yourself regarding your finances, and some issues that you will need to plan for. These will help you decide how you need to plan your finances for future investments.

What return will I get?

In order to be able to calculate your gross yield from a property, you will have to decide what rental you will reasonably be able to charge your tenants. Gross yield is calculated by dividing the annual gross rental by the price you pay for the property. Compare the resulting yield that you will earn with the interest rate that you could get if your money was in the bank.

Keep in mind that holiday homes will not be able to generate a return if you are not willing to rent it out. Also, unless you can keep your holiday home occupied throughout the year, they will only be able to generate an income when they are occupied during the holiday season.

Is my property going to produce a positive cash flow?

We've talked about cash flow in a previous chapter, and how it is imperative to have a profitable property investment career. The ultimate goal when investing in real estate is having your property produce income for you, especially as you draw closer to your retirement. Your primary motivation for purchasing a property should be so that it makes you money, not so much as because it saves you tax.

It is also quite meaningless to acquire great amounts of debt to purchase a property that you think might increase in value. The value of a property might not appreciate the way that you expected it would, or at the rate that you were expecting.

What if interest rates go up or I lose a tenant?

You will need to ensure that you're able to pay the bond and all other expenses like taxes and rates if your tenant moves out and you aren't able to find a new one for a few months. You've got to be able to afford the bond repayments if the bond rates go up by 3 or 4%. Working this out as soon as you can is vital, as these things can seriously affect your cash flow.

Am I prepared to sell my property if necessary?

An exit strategy is always required for cases where you need to back out of an investment. Unfortunately, there is no time to be sentimental about properties in this industry, and you will have to be fully prepared to sell if the situation becomes dire, and you have to move on.

How many properties can I afford?

It's important to figure out how many properties you will be able to afford based on how you went about financing the acquisition of your first investment property. It's so easy to get swept up with the excitement that comes with buying investment real estate, but you have to consider options only that are affordable and will not put you in any sticky financial situations.

Am I prepared to manage an investment?

As with any investment, property investments need to be managed carefully and properly. You need to think about whether you want to be the sole manager of a property, or whether you want to hire a property manager to take care of it for you. As we've said a few times, property managers are expensive, but they are an excellent investment, especially for those who own a number of properties in different locations. They are great for relieving some of the stress that comes with owning and managing investment properties.

As you can see, there are a lot of things that you need to do to manage your investments properly. Asking the above questions is a vital step that every investor should take before committing their funds to a property, and you should be aware that assessing the performance of your investments on an annual basis is a must.

It's also highly beneficial to educate yourself about the advantages and drawbacks of any kind of investment before you spend any of your money.

Chapter Eight:

Mistakes You Can and Should

Avoid

You can't expect to become an expert in real estate investing overnight. Yes, there is good money to be made buying, renting, and selling properties, but doing so takes knowledge, skill, and a lot of determination. While we all know that failure is the best way to learn, it's usually better to learn from other peoples' mistakes rather than make them yourself.

Knowing some of the classic mistakes that other investors make with their properties can help you avoid making them. In this chapter, we are going to discuss some of the most common and often most detrimental mistakes that rookie property investors make, and how you can avoid them.

Failure to plan

You're probably sick of being told that you need to plan, but I cannot stress it enough. The last thing you ever want to do is acquire a property and then figure out what you want to do with it afterward. Resisting the buying frenzy can feel impossible when the market is heated, but it is crucial that you resist the temptation.

Decide on an investment strategy, like one of those that were outlined in *Chapter Three,* before you put in the cash or get a mortgage. Consider the type of property you're looking for. Do you want it to be a vacation destination? A family home? If so, should it be single-family or multi-family? Decide on a plan for purchasing, and then find properties that line up with your plan.

Appreciation-based investments

This is perhaps the most common mistake that investors tend to make. Many people tend to invest in real estate based on the idea that its value will appreciate in the following years. There are a few reasons why this is a terrible idea. Rental property values can and will fluctuate each year, and houses might plummet in value during a down market.

As an investor, you might be required to sell your property unexpectedly, and, when done in a bad market, can cause massive losses. Instead, choose to invest based on a property's cash flow. This is why you need to have a strong idea of the numbers during the investigation process for buying a rental property you intend to keep in your portfolio.

The person that you are buying the property from should be able to give you at least one year's worth of *verifiable* rental numbers *in writing* when you are considering a property to purchase.

Lack of research

Normally, before someone buys a car, they compare different models, ask plenty of questions, and figure out whether it is worth their cash. This same mentality should be applied to purchasing a home but on a far more thorough level. Your research should also be based on the type of investor that you want to be, such as a landlord, a flipper, or a land developer.

In addition to asking a lot of questions regarding the potential property, you should ask about the neighborhood that the property is in as well. Things like nearby commercial or construction sites, known flood zones, replacement fixtures, and crime threats should all be things you inquire about before buying real estate.

Incomplete contracts

When I say 'incomplete', I don't mean contracts that are unfinished, but rather ones that are not comprehensive enough. You should always cover all of your assumptions in the contract when you buy a rental property and be sure to read through them rigorously. When you purchase a property, you're going to have to sign several contracts.

Each of these contracts and real estate partnership agreements need to be read very carefully before you even think of signing them. Missing items can end up costing you a lot of money to fix, and you might even need to contact your lawyer to rectify the problem. It's better to get the contract exactly the way you want it before it's signed, and possibly even hire a lawyer to guide you through this process.

Doing everything alone

A common misconception that buyers tend to have is that they can close a real estate transaction on their own, or that they know it all. Even if you have completed a few deals previously that went well, the process may not be as smooth when the market is down, and there won't be anyone you can call on for help if you want to remedy a property deal that is not ideal.

As a property investor, you should tap into every resource at your disposal, and network with experts that will be able to help you make the best purchases. Your list of potential experts should include people like handymen, home inspectors, real estate agents, and a good attorney. Experts in these fields will be able to fill you in on any flaws that a neighborhood may have.

Inadequate insurance

Insurance is one of the most important aspects of property investments. Having good, comprehensive insurance will help ensure that your investments are protected in case they become damaged from bad weather, like hurricanes or floods. Taking out insurance that isn't tailored to your needs, or not taking out any insurance at all, is another extremely common mistake that investors make.

Choosing the right insurance is just as important as choosing an investment property, and should be carefully considered when buying a rental property. Your insurance policy needs to take into account all of the factors that are specific to your situation, including your financial state and where the property is located.

Overpayment

This is a problem somewhat linked to that of not doing enough research. Finding good real estate to invest in is exhausting, frustrating, and time-consuming. Rookie investors tend to be too hasty to accept the first offer that is made to them when they finally find a property because they do not want to have to keep searching.

The problem with this is that investors will tend to overpay for properties. Doing so can lead to a domino effect of problems in the future. You might end up overextending yourself and accumulating too much debt, which leads to more expensive payments that you won't be able to afford.

The result is a battle to recoup your investment that could last years. If you want to determine whether or not the price tag on a property is too steep, you should find out the prices that other homes in the area have sold for. Real estate brokers can assist you and give you the information that you need without much hassle at all.

Or you could take a look at some of the prices of comparable properties in the local newspaper, or in real estate databases. Unless a home has some unique features that would cause its value to appreciate over time, you should do your best to have your bids be consistent with the other property sales in the area.

Even if you can't reach an agreement with the seller, there will always be other opportunities - something that investors sometimes forget. The chances are that there will be another place out there that is exactly what you're looking for, and for a favorable price as well. Just be patient.

Underestimated expenses

There's a lot more to owning property than merely paying the mortgage, which is something that novice real estate investors tend to forget. There are costs that come with the upkeep of a property and making sure that home appliances like the refrigerator, oven, washer, and dryer are functioning properly. Not to mention the cost of making structural changes to the building.

The best thing to do is to create a list of every monthly expense you will need to pay for maintaining and running the property. In the case of rentals, once you have added the numbers up and you have included the monthly rent, you can calculate the Return On Investment that will help you figure out if your income will cover the cost of maintenance and mortgage. Below is an example of what such a list should look like:

Mortgage	$22 000
Electricity	$150
Water	$80
Lawn service	$50
Appliances	$500

The values above are fabricated but are there to give you an idea of what your list could contain. Determining these expenses before you purchase a house is essential for house flippers as well since your profits will be tied directly to the time it takes to buy the home, renovate it, and resell it. Regardless, as an investor, developing one of these lists is vital.

You will also need to focus on the short-term costs for financing, cancellation fees, and repayment penalties that might incur when the house is flipped.

Buying too many properties

Like we said in the previous chapter, it's easy to get caught up in a buying frenzy during good markets, especially for first-time investors. It's a good idea to acquire one property so that you can get a feel for the industry. You should also always remember that buying a rental property is a much different experience than buying your first home.

Even if you've already bought your first home, buying a property for the purpose of investment is a totally different process and experience. In nearly all cases, you would be better off buying just one property to start off with. Doing this gives you a good idea of the process and involvement that investing in property requires.

If you can, you should wait at least one year before you purchase any additional properties. This will give you more than enough time to learn and understand everything that owning and managing your own rental property entails. This time frame also lets you work out any issues that you may run into. Think of your first investment property as an opportunity to learn the business of real estate ownership, and to understand it better.

These are all of the main problems that new investors encounter when they enter the industry. Now that you know what they are, and understand what they can cause, avoiding them should be a walk in the park. Be sure to take all of the advice in this chapter into consideration!

Chapter Nine:

Expanding Your Horizons

The logical next step for investors who have made their first investment property purchase is to acquire more properties. Many property investors have portfolios that consist only of one or two properties, because they don't know how to manage a larger portfolio - at least not the right way.

But why do investors avoid buying more than three properties? Well, how many properties do you think you could afford if each of them cost you $1000 a month to own. Unless you are earning more than $200 000 every year, the right answer is 'not a lot.'

You only have so much disposable income to spend on property, and since most investors purchase properties that they have to pay for each month, you quickly deplete your disposable income. So, how are you going to acquire more real estate and expand your portfolio?

That's what we'll be discussing in this chapter.

Leverage your current equity growth

If you already own one or two properties, then you have the ability to speed up your property growth by leveraging the equity that you have in them. Trying to save up your deposits is a very slow and arduous process. If you can use the wealth that your current portfolio has accumulated to acquire more real estate, then you will be able to expand your portfolio at a much faster rate.

For example, if you were to buy a property for $300 000 and assume that its value would appreciate to $400 000, then you would have an effective $100 000 equity in that property. This equity would only be available in two ways: you could either sell the property to receive the cash that is left over ($100 000 minus expenses) or you could borrow money against the equity (generally to a maximum of 80%, which would be $80 000).

Using your equity means that you will not need to put any money from your pockets towards buying more properties. The equity from your current properties is used to pay for the deposit. The more properties you buy, the quicker your equity will increase, which will allow you to acquire more properties.

Generate a positive cash flow

Not being able to afford the repayments for service on a property is one of the main reasons that investors do not purchase more real estate. In other words, they purchase property that costs them money, instead of property that makes them money, meaning that they are limiting themselves with how much property they could afford.

Having each of your properties generate a cash flow that is positive would mean that your investments would pay you to own them. You would receive a payout each month that is more than the sum of your expenses, which you could then use to spend, or better yet, invest, to your heart's delight.

Purchasing properties with a positive cash flow has a domino effect - the more positive cash flow properties you own, the more properties you will be able to afford. You are essentially increasing your total disposable income with each property you acquire by increasing the amount of passive income that you earn. Your disposable income is not being decreased like it would be if you were investing in properties that had negative cash flows.

Without cash flow, you can't afford to own, let alone buy, property.

Be able to assess the market quickly

Every great investor with multiple properties in their portfolio is able to scan the market for good deals in the shortest amount of time possible. You need to keep an eye on the market at all times, but you also need to be able to find those hidden gems that will make you a fortune hastily and with ease.

There are a number of tools online that will help you do this. They allow you to find properties that are geared positively easily and quickly, as well as those that are undervalued, require renovating, or ones from buyers

Investigate + research current market.

that are willing to negotiate a favorable deal. If you choose not to use one of these tools, then you will need to come up with your own way of scanning the market.

Up the value of your current properties

Increasing the value of your properties and their rental incomes is the best way to increase your cash flow and generate more disposable income that can be put towards buying more real estate. This can be done by doing minor and some major renovations to the properties that are currently in your portfolio. A new carpet and a fresh coat of paint will do wonders for the value of your properties.

Don't avoid purchasing properties that are fixer-uppers. These properties are usually the ones that are sold for the lowest prices. Doing some small renovations to such properties will drastically increase their value, which will subsequently increase the amount of money in your pocket each month.

Adding value will increase the rate at which you are able to buy new properties.

Monitor your portfolio closely

It goes without saying that your properties are not going to take care of themselves unless you hire a property manager. Even then, you will need to keep an eye on them to make sure that everything is running smoothly.

You can think of your real estate like a child - if they are left unmonitored, they will cause damage to themselves and the things around them, especially in the early stages. The same things are true for the properties in your portfolio. You will need to monitor them and guide them to improvement and growth. Merely acquiring property and expecting it to take care of itself is the best way to ensure that you're never able to buy another property again.

Look at the finances of your properties and make sure that they are accurate. Monitor their conditions and talk to real estate agents and home improvement companies about things that you can do to increase their value.

Screen your tenants carefully, choose them wisely, and make sure that they are paying their rent on time and doing some basic property maintenance. Also, pay attention to your property manager if you have one - if they aren't doing their job properly, or just suck in general, sack them.

Combine positive cash flow with rapid growth

If all of your properties are experiencing rapid appreciation of value, but are not producing a positive cash flow, then you will find that you will be unable to afford to pay your loans. On the other hand, if all of your properties are producing a positive cash flow, but are not experiencing any capital growth, then you are at risk of having no equity that you can use to invest in new real estate.

Your perfect personal combination of rapid growth and positive cash flow is going to depend on your time frame and risk profile. If your goal is to retire in five years, then you will probably want to avoid a property that is geared negatively and instead opt for the cash

94

flow. But, if you are still young and are looking to expand your portfolio quickly and you are happy in your current job, then you likely won't bother with pulling income from your real estate at this point.

In that case, you will want to balance the number of positive cash flow and rapid growth properties that you purchase. This will allow you to be geared neutrally, meaning you won't be out of money, but can still achieve a desirable growth in equity to speed up the growth of your portfolio.

When it's time, do damage control

Don't flog a dead horse' as the old saying goes. The same idea applies to investments that are not bringing in any money. Too often, property investors will maintain a dead investment because they do not want to admit that they have made a loss or acquired a bad investment. They are also too afraid to lose money, so they continue to hold onto properties even when their value drops. Some even keep real estate for over ten years before it returns to its original value, then claim that they 'haven't lost any money.'

Have an investment strategy

Bet you thought you'd read the word 'plan' for the last time two chapters ago. Nope! Planning will never not be important, even when you are buying your 100th property. Knowing your strategy for investment will allow you to form a list of ideas for things you want from your properties.

This will make the property-buying process much easier. You'll be able to narrow your market from every property out there to only the ones that fit into your investment strategy and suit you the best. You end up wasting far less time, and you will generate income faster, which lets you grow your portfolio quickly as well.

Growing your portfolio is an important step that every new property investor needs to take. It is the key to generating more income, which is the goal for most of us. Following the steps mentioned in this chapter will get you growing your portfolio faster than you could ever have imagined, as long as you remain motivated and determined.

Wrapping Up

We've said it time and time again throughout the course of this book, and we'll say it again: being a property investor is not easy. There is a ton of work involved, and you have to be prepared to take on all of the risks and responsibilities that this industry comes with.

But, if you are determined, motivated, and hardworking, you will be able to achieve your financial goals before you know it - and this book will get you there. Whether you are a novice investor just entering the market, or a real estate professional with hundreds of properties to your name, there is something to be learned from this guide for everyone.

If there's one thing to take away from this book, it's that anyone is capable of making their dreams a reality, regardless of their upbringings or backgrounds. Now get out there and get investing!

Disclaimer

The opinions and ideas of the author contained in this publication are designed to educate the reader in an informative and helpful manner. While we accept that the instructions will not suit every reader, it is only to be expected that the recipes might not gel with everyone. Use the book responsibly and at your own risk. This work with all its contents, does not guarantee correctness, completion, quality or correctness of the provided information. Always check with your medical practitioner should you be unsure whether to follow a low carb eating plan. Misinformation or misprints cannot be completely eliminated. Human error is real!

Design: NataliaDesign

Picture: **bookzv**/ www.shutterstock.com

Printed in Great Britain
by Amazon